THATCHER

GRAPHIC GUIDES
Series editor: Philip Boys

Apartheid
Donald Woods & Mike Bostock

Thatcher
Ed Harriman & John Freeman

Space Wars
Martin Ince & David Hine

Women Artists
Frances Borzello & Natacha Ledwidge

Forthcoming titles

Broadcasting
Peter Lewis & Corinne Pearlman

Language
Rob Pope & Graham Higgins

THATCHER
A GRAPHIC GUIDE

Text: Ed Harriman
Illustrations: John Freeman

CAMDEN PRESS

Published in 1986 by
Camden Press Ltd
43 Camden Passage, London N1 8EB, England

Text © Ed Harriman
Illustrations © John Freeman
Designed by John Maddison

Set in 11 on 13 pt Bookman Light
By Windhorse Photosetters
247 Globe Road, Bethnal Green, London E2
and printed and bound in Great Britain by
A. Wheaton & Co. Ltd, Exeter

British Library CIP Data
Harriman, Ed
    Thatcher: a graphic guide. — (Graphic guides)
    1. Thatcher, Margaret   2. Prime ministers —
    Great Britain — Biography
    I. Title   II. Series
    941.085′7′0924   DA591.T47

ISBN 0 948491 02 7(pb)

OCTOBER 13, 1925. In a small front room above a grocery store in Grantham, Lincolnshire, Margaret Hilda Roberts is born.

Her father, Alfred Roberts, the son of a shoemaker, had recently set up in the grocery business.

Her mother, Beatrice, had been a seamstress. Her father was the cloakroom attendant at the railway station.

Britain slept.

Fifty four years later – Margaret Thatcher became Britain's first woman Prime Minister.

'I came to office with one deliberate intent: to change Britain from a dependent to a self-reliant society; from a give-it-to-me to a do-it-yourself nation; a get-up-and-go instead of a sit-back-and-wait-for-it Britain.'

Brave words.

But since then National output – oil aside – hasn't grown at all.

Unemployment is the highest ever.

Britain as an economy has actually shrunk compared to other Western nations.

'As a personality who has an absolute passion for getting things right for Britain, I just can't bear Britain in decline.'

A lot of people 'just can't bear' Margaret Thatcher. Can you blame them?

In industrial towns up and down the country factories are boarded up and a night's entertainment is likely to be a trip to the chip shop.

Outside hospitals nurses shake tins collecting donations to buy bedpans.

Even in the suburbs there are executives and managers who now count themselves lucky to have jobs tending gardens.

Britain has become a land of dole queues. And Margaret Thatcher's chosen to be a very special type of leader. In August 1985, as unemployment touched 3¼ million, she and her husband Denis announced they were now owners of a £400,000 home in a London suburb.

'Most people would think it right that those who are in work should be better off than those who unfortunately cannot find work.'

She always said she would lead by example.

THE SORRY STATE

A century ago London was the largest city in the world, the centre of world trade. Britain had the highest standard of living and its manufacturing cities were the cores of the world's most productive industries. Its Empire was world-wide. Yet soon after the Great 1851 Crystal Palace Exhibition, steel and coal production in both Germany and the United States surpassed Britain's. Since then the British economy has been in relative decline.

It has been, by and large, a gentle, gentlemanly slide.

Through the City of London wealth was pumped overseas into new businesses and opportunities. British industry grew old, worn out. Dead wood accumulated in the board rooms and ancient machinery in the factories; there was massive overmanning.

Innovation was left to the elbow benders quaffing pints in working men's clubs, or downing gin and tonics at golf club bars.

When Margaret Thatcher became Prime Minister in 1979 she said she was going to change all that. She'd make Britain prosperous again. But that wasn't new. Harold Wilson had said he'd do the same when he first became Labour Prime Minister in the 1960s.

But Margaret Thatcher was different. She was also going to rid the country of socialism. Bury it. Forever.

The post-war economic policies of both Labour and Tory governments had demonstrably failed, she said. Worse than that, the nation was being subverted.

'We are witnessing a deliberate attack on our values... on those who want to promote merit and excellence... on our heritage and our great past,'

she told the Tory Conference in 1975. And what exactly did that mean?

'Nations depend for their health upon the achievements of a comparatively small number of talented and determined people... It was not possible for many of these talented people to believe that we valued them when we maintained penal tax rates, decade after decade, in order to please those who seemed to be motivated mainly by envy.'

Margaret Thatcher would make sure the 'talented people' felt cared for when she became Prime Minister.

She'd give them a big hug.

This may not seem terribly high-minded. But it was exhilarating stuff to men in the City, tired Tories looking for lost passion, and young working class couples roaring around the surburbs in new Ford Cortinas. They, like her, saw no reason why the state should care for the 'undeserving'. She also delivered what they wanted – the promise of limitless consumer goods.

Where a few years ago stood factories, there are now bulldozed vacant lots. And new prefabricated warehouses, crammed with what the Sunday colour magazines depict as icons of good living. And all available on easy credit terms:
televisions
washing machines
videos
automobiles
refrigerators
computers.

The trouble is that most of these are imported. In fact, over £60 billion worth of consumer goods have been imported in the past seven years. And precious few pennies from them have gone into British industry, money which was going to make Britain 'Great' again.

13

'We didn't promise you instant sunshine,' she said soon after taking office.

And as for the unemployed?

'One in eight of our people is unemployed — far, far too many — but seven out of eight are in fact working.'

HANDBAG ECONOMICS

Margaret Thatcher talks a great deal about the need for law and order, hard work and a return to Victorian values. Nonetheless, for her economics has been *the* crucial issue. Before she became leader of the Conservative Party she aspired to be Chancellor of the Exchequer.

'My policies are based not on some economic theory but on the things I and millions like me were brought up with. An honest day's pay; live within your means; put by a nest egg for a rainy day; pay your bills on time; support the police.'

But wait a minute.

Households don't run on strictly balanced budgets, now do they? It's hire purchase, mortgages and all sorts of credit... Access and Barclaycard, an overdraft at the bank and piles of unpaid bills.

And life on many of Britain's housing estates could hardly be more different. There the 'nest egg's' likely to be in the gas meter, for which you need a jemmy. Half the block's probably not paid its rent or rates for months. The only jobs going are driving mini-cabs or pushing dope. And as for supporting the police...

But does that really matter?

Margaret Thatcher made economics sound easy, and anyone who can do that deserves to be popular. Yet even so she didn't talk to bankers about handbags and grocery lists. They were offered a richer brew; something a bit esoteric, a shade mystical, and apparently new . . .

Monetarism.

Monetarism's wonderfully simple. It's foolish of governments to intervene in the economy, monetarists say. In fact it's worse than foolish, it's disastrous. Because as far as monetarists are concerned everything and everyone's life in the end is determined by the free market.

So chuck out welfare policies, Keynesian deficit spending

and concepts such as social responsibility. And don't ask too many questions about how the hallowed free market is supposed to survive in a world dominated by international banks, multinational corporations and what US President Eisenhower once called 'the military-industrial complex'.

The tricky bits can be left to monetarism's own intellectuals.

For businessmen and bankers, monetarism had gut appeal — government's hands off and noses out of their commercial affairs, and a guarantee that the so-called public interest would not be funded out of their profits.

And what they liked about Margaret Thatcher was that she thumped their drum, preaching monetarism with the fervour of a religious convert.

Monetarists said chop 'runaway' government spending because, if not, the government has to print more money (which they say leads to inflation) or collect more taxes (which reduces profits).

Margaret Thatcher talked of government spending as the sure road to hellfire and damnation.

Monetarists said that government's prime responsibility was to control inflation.

Margaret Thatcher talked of inflation as if it was crucifying all that was decent in British life.

'Inflation is the biggest destroyer of all — of industry, of jobs, of savings, of society . . . Unless we elevate the reduction of inflation to a first priority the very fabric of society will fall apart.'

The problem, of course, was how to control inflation. All over the world, governments of all political stripes had tried, but most had become unstuck.

Again monetarism offered a quick and easy answer. It goes as follows:

1. The rate of inflation is inextricably linked to the growth of the money supply. Don't ask monetarists how they are linked because they've always had problems proving that one. Just take it as given.

2. The money supply is all the cash and credit in the banking system and your purse or trouser pockets.

3. Now monetarists say the government has one very simple lever by which it can control the money supply, and that's through the Bank of England in its daily dealings with the commercial banks.

4. So all the government has to do is issue strict instructions to the Bank of England to follow policies which reduce the amount of money in circulation, and

HEY PRESTO!

Inflation will have to fall.

Marvellous, isn't it?

Margaret Thatcher thought so, and told everybody what a good idea it was. She also said she would simply tot up all the government's spending, set it alongside the government's revenue from taxes, asset sales and other sources. And then make sure the balance the government had to borrow – the so-called Public Spending Borrowing Requirement – kept coming down.

Is it any surprise businessmen loved her?

Margaret Thatcher, of course, had her critics. A few quick jottings on the back of an envelope, they said, and anyone would realise that if public expenditure is cut then people are going to be thrown out of work, not least among them public employees, such as teachers, nurses and dustmen. And businesses dependent on state contracts would also suffer.

In other words, monetarism was just a fancy new excuse for a massive old-fashioned deflationary squeeze. And as with all such squeezes, every point off the rate of inflation could be read off on a pocket calculator in bankruptcies and lost jobs.

They also said that the last time Britain went through such a economic nightmare was during the Depression of the 1930s, when it took the Nazi invasion of half of Europe to get the British arms industries going and the economy back on its feet again.

Never one to give critics much quarter, Margaret Thatcher quickly dismissed them.

'There is absolutely no comparison between today and the 1930s, none whatsoever.'

So there. And as for the bankruptcies and unemployed, Margaret Thatcher never said it would be easy. She just said,

'THERE IS NO ALTERNATIVE'.

'You turn if you want to, the lady's not for turning.'

21

Tory stalwarts loved it. But many people in Britain, among them men and women deeply experienced in government and finance, let alone those just trying to make a living, never shared her view. They were to be ignored.

Margaret Thatcher offered something else as well: a real clincher. If 'Socialism' is the greatest evil and impediment to so-called 'sound government' in Britain, then the greatest threat to 'free enterprise' is the unions – the people who 'hold the nation to ransom' demanding 'unrealistically high' wages for producing goods which can't be sold either here or abroad.

Again Margaret Thatcher took the grumblings from corporate boardrooms – indeed, of men such as her husband Denis – and projected them as high blown moral imperatives. Attacking unions has for years been a popular blood sport in Britain.

'There are people in this country who are great destroyers; they wish to destroy the kind of free society we have... **Many of these people are in the unions.'**

Many businessmen found monetarism just so much mumbo-jumbo. But they certainly warmed to the old girl's fighting spirit, stumping up hundreds of thousands of pounds towards the 1979 and 1983 election campaigns to get her into office.

Trafalgar House
Taylor Woodrow
United Biscuits
Plessey
Trust House Forte
Rank Organisation
GKN
Consolidated Goldfields, Racal, Hanson Trust...

Most of the big firms and lots of tiddlers chipped in. It was a small price to pay for the 'new era of realism' she promised, of free enterprise unfettered by state controls and union bosses.

'For the first time in 40 years you can decide simultaneously what to pay your employees, what to charge for your goods, what dividend to pay on capital and what to invest overseas.'

Profits and competitiveness would be restored.
Investment would come pouring back into industry.
The 'Great' would again be back in front of 'Britain', where it belonged.

OOOPS!

It hasn't happened.

Why not? After all, wages are now 'realistically' low. The unions have been hobbled and hundreds of thousands of people are literally begging for jobs.

The answer's not terribly complicated. Margaret Thatcher bungled. Her economic policies don't work, as hundreds of Britain's top economists had been saying all along. Shortly after her election, she also abolished exchange controls.

'Whoopie!'

Since then anyone – holiday maker, industrialist, banker, train robber – has been able to change sterling into any other currency, in any amount, at any time, and get it out of the country.

And they have.

Margaret Thatcher once said that the aim of Conservative policy is **'the furtherance of remarkable people.'**

'Sounds good to me.'

'Remarkable people' have indeed done rather well under Margaret Thatcher. But they haven't shown themselves terribly keen on the hard slog to profitability managing small engineering firms in the Midlands, or setting up microchip industries outside Glasgow; the sort of enterprise for which Prince Albert and other eminent Victorians would have admired them.

Their buzz word instead is 'convertibility.'

Get wealth out of fixed assets — such as factories and offices, which are heavy on overheads and responsibilities such as paying the workers and repairing the toilets — and into liquid assets, fast.

Into cash and negotiable instruments which can be shifted all over the world, wherever the promise of quick returns beckons.

Overnight US Treasury loans, short term investments, Japanese electronics shares, and currency dealing. Or just stash it in a bank in an offshore tax haven. In other words, strip the shop and hoof it overseas.

If you are a company treasurer, how attractive it can be to shut down factories at home.

'Sorry, lads. Sorry, ladies. There's no money in the till.'

Then open up subsidiaries in Third World countries where labour is cheap and plentiful, and police have few sensitivities about civil liberties.

'Our firm is becoming much more international.'

In the first year after she abolished exchange controls some £3 billion in portfolio investments fled overseas through banks, brokerage houses, pension funds and some of Britain's largest corporations.

Since she became Prime Minister the figure has risen to over £40 billion.

Add to that Britain's first ever manufacturing trade deficit of £9 billion over the last three years.

And the £32 billion paid to people on the dole.

That's over £80 billion.

Spent differently it could have created a lot of jobs, built a lot of factories, paid a lot of wages, and possibly even provided a whole new way of life for many British families. Instead, millions of women today listen to radio disc jockeys telling them how lucky they are to be at home doing the laundry.

Their old man's gone fishing for the third time in a week. The daughter stays out all night. And the kid comes home from the football drunk and bruised, and won't talk about it.

No politician seriously believes that jobs will ever be found for at least half the unemployed. But they don't say so. There are no votes in it. Such is Margaret Thatcher's Britain.

'This country belongs to the courageous, not the timid.'

How did it happen?

By the time she was 12 little Margaret Roberts had a clear vision of the world. All wisdom came from her father, Alfred.

'He brought me up to believe all the things I do believe, and they're the values on which I fought the election. I owe almost everything to my father.'

Beatrice, her mother, worked long hours in the home and shop. When she baked she gave a loaf to poor neighbours. But her daughter found her wanting.

'I love my mother dearly but after I was fifteen we had nothing more to say to each other. It wasn't her fault. She was weighed down by the home, always being in the home.'

Margaret also had an older sister, Muriel. Today Muriel is a farmer's wife. Margaret seldom mentions her. Margaret was Daddy's Girl. Family savings went to pay for her elocution and Latin lessons.

'Some of us were making it long before Woman's Lib was ever thought of.'

While Beatrice worked, Margaret and Alfred Roberts were out canvassing together. Alfred was an active Methodist, a Conservative-leaning Independent councillor, then alderman, and later Grantham's mayor.

It was the depths of the Depression.

Alfred's views were austere.

Margaret learned that the righteous prosper, and the poor get what they deserve. People slept in cardboard boxes in the slums next to Alfred Roberts's grocery store.

But there was no room for compassion behind the counter. Alfred wanted paying customers, not penniless neighbours. Margaret was sent to school with the children of the 'better sort of people' from the nicer part of town.

'You worked hard, not because work was everything, but because work was necessary to give you what you wanted. There was also a feeling that idleness was waste.'

It's a nice picture. But it's not quite true.

Alfred Roberts was a determined man, but his success was not entirely due to his own endeavours. He had a little outside help.

Alfred didn't just run the grocery store. There was a sub-post office at the end of the counter. So while many nearby corner shops went bankrupt, Alfred Roberts's didn't. The sub-post office provided a guaranteed income – and customers. People recollect that Alfred would 'put an extra penny on the bacon, you know, that sort of thing,' because he knew they would have to come into his shop to post their weekly coupons for the football pools.

Pensioners were guaranteed customers. Having collected their ten shilling pensions at one end of the counter, they paid cash for groceries before they got out of the door.

Margaret Thatcher hardly ever mentions this – her own family's debt to state support. That its business success – in a climate of extreme competition and depression – was due in no small measure to its local monopoly on state services.

Nonetheless, Alfred was determined that Margaret would succeed. She would survive the depression within her family, hardly sharing her feelings or experiences with anyone, let alone with her poor neighbours or school mates.

'I was a very serious child . . . There was not a lot of fun or sparkle in my life.'

In school she studied hard. Her teachers said she had little imagination. But through sheer repetition, long hours and application she learned her lessons well. Well enough to go to Oxford.

OXFORD & SWISS ROLLS

From 1943 to 1947 Margaret Roberts was a student at Somerville College, Oxford.

She found Oxford difficult, especially at first. It was full of snobs; they found her hopelessly gauche, her accent wildly affected.

And she had opinions on everything, which got up her classmates' noses. They were for the most part Daddy's opinions, and she seems never to have tired of voicing them, loudly and often. Margaret was studying chemistry.

'She was a good beta, hardworking, competent. None of us ever thought she would go very far,' said Dame Janet Vaughan, Somerville's principal.

But she was also busy elsewhere, at the one place at Oxford where she was free to sound off – the Oxford University Conservative Association. In 1946 they made her president, a post she held for two years.

NEECE HICE. PWETEH HET, MEH NEMS MEGEHRET

And she found a heart throb, the son of an Earl. He took her home to meet his mother. She disapproved, and Margaret was dropped.

The experience is said to have wounded her deeply.

Her passions were channelled elsewhere:

'I suppose I was about 20, and a crowd of us had been to a village hop and came back to make midnight cups of coffee. I was in the kitchen helping to dish up and having a fierce argument with one of the boys in the crowd when someone else interrupted to say: "Of course, Margaret, you will go in for politics, won't you?" I stopped dead. Suddenly it was crystallised for me. I knew.'

In 1947 Margaret left Oxford with a second class degree. She found a job in a small industrial laboratory, British Xylonite Plastics Ltd, fifty miles from London in Colchester. She did well. She was a 'blue stocking' chemist; workers called her 'Duchess'.

Then she took a job working on fillings for Swiss rolls with J. Lyons and Co. in the London borough of Hammersmith.

A young woman of slender means, she saved her good clothes for weekends, when she hung around Tory meetings.

'There are times when I've been desperately unhappy and disappointed. I knocked about a bit, as they say.'

Hanging about finally paid off. At the annual party conference in 1948 she bumped into the director of Blackwell's Bookshop in Oxford, who remembered her. He suggested to a chum, the Conservative agent for Dartford, an industrial town near London, that Margaret might make a passable candidate.

The Dartford Conservative Association took her on.

In the late 1940s Labour was in power, and Churchill was fast losing his grip. Dartford was a safe Labour seat so it was a foregone conclusion that Margaret would lose the 1950 and 1951 elections.

But there was a consolation prize...

Denis!

Denis Thatcher was then 36 years old, a Methodist, and managing director of a modestly successful sheep dip and pesticide company founded by his grandfather. Denis had had an averagely eventful war in the Royal Artillery. He'd been married, but divorced his wife shortly after.

'When I came back from the war, my wife and I were strangers.'

Basically Denis was a bit of a gent who wanted to settle down, as long as he could keep his rugby and golfing cronies and bend the occasional elbow at the bar. He had respectably large quantities of money, a comfortable little flat in Chelsea, and he drove a Jaguar.

'It is expensive to be in politics. One has to be so mobile, one has to be well groomed, and one has to entertain.'

They were married on December 13, 1951. Since then Denis has played the loving fool. As he said:

'Who could meet Margaret without being completely slain by her personality and intellectual brilliance?'

As the benefits of marrying a businessman began to accrue, Margaret Thatcher and Dartford drew apart.

They set up house in Chelsea. She had twins, Mark and Carol, in 1953. They hired a live-in nanny.

The twins were went to public schools. The family moved to a large home in Farnborough, a London stockbroker suburb.

'A medium-sized house with five bedrooms standing in one and a half acres of gardens. We have an excellent daily help who keeps the house in spotless order. Nannie looks after the children's rooms and their clothes.'

Denis had paid for Margaret to study law. She qualified and practised, but she had great difficulty finding a place in chambers. Denis's support and her own obstinacy sustained her.

In 1959 she won the parliamentary seat for Finchley, a comfortable north London borough. It was a safe Conservative seat. She could become a full-time politician at last. Overnight she became the Grande Dame of raffle parties, church fêtes and frilly hats, as she lunged into constituency activities with alarming intensity.

By her own account Margaret was busy, busy, busy. And a devoted mother.

'Of course the children do become the centre of your life and you live for them as you'd never lived for anyone else... **and yet I knew that I had something more to give.'**

Her biographer, Penny Junor, tells a slightly different story.

She'd telephone home to say 'Good Night', often not seeing her children in the evenings at all. They weren't allowed to have pets. She had little time to play with them at weekends.

And she never told them their father had been married before.

Mark and Carol only found out in 1976. They read it in the newspapers. Penny Junor says their mother was 'devastated'. Why hadn't she told them?

'One didn't keep it a secret he'd been married before. One wasn't asked. One just didn't talk about a thing like that.'

At least, not in the Thatcher household.

THE BORING YEARS

In 1961 Prime Minister Harold MacMillan gave Margaret Thatcher a small job as Parliamentary Secretary in the Ministry of Pensions. 'You've never had it so good,' MacMillan told the nation.

Yet three years later the Tories lost the General Election to Harold Wilson and the Labour Party. For the rest of the decade Margaret Thatcher was shuffled around the parliamentary opposition.

Edward Heath, the new Tory leader, made her opposition spokesperson on Housing. Then he moved her to Treasury. In 1967 he brought her into his shadow cabinet as shadow minister for Power. The next year he moved her to Education. She was determined and hard-working, but her performance was lacklustre. So she decided to give a speech about what she stood for.

It was a long-winded affair, delivered at a fringe meeting at the Conservative Annual Conference in Blackpool in 1968.

'I believe that the great mistake of the last few years has been for the government to provide or to legislate for almost everything . . . As a result people no longer feel important in the scheme of things . . . There is no room for the individual, his talents, his requirements or his wishes. He no longer counts.'

The press all but ignored her.

Nonetheless, when Ted Heath and the Conservatives won the 1970 general election Margaret Thatcher got her ministry. She became Secretary of State for Education. It was her first public office, one for which she had slogged for nearly twenty years. She soon established a reputation.

'I took the view that most parents are able to pay for the milk for their children.'

So she scrapped free milk for primary school children. The press wasn't impressed.

'Cave Woman', 'Milk Snatcher', they called her. Free school milk had been a tangible sign of the government's concern for Britain's children. A promise that Britain wouldn't slide back to the desperate 1930s. A symbol of what millions of soldiers and women had voted for at the end of the Second World War. In other words, a sacred cow.

But Margaret Thatcher saw it as part of a greater scourge.

'We almost sacrificed everything in that war. Then we had Socialism, and it bit very deep into Britain — it bit deep throughout society.'

If the kids got a free pinta today, then they'd expect roast beef and all the trimmings tomorrow.

The press, the public and her colleagues disowned her. So she tried to undo the damage by spelling out to the nation the logic of her own grocery shopping.

'With my husband facing retirement I see prices rise, so one builds up a quiet store of food and household things that one hopes one will need . . . What you collect are the expensive proteins: ham, tongue, salmon, mackerel, sardines. They will last for years. I've got some corned beef too.'

Labour jumped all over her, gleeful. This was hoarding, they said, commodity speculation in the larder. More to the point it didn't seem to have dawned on the Secretary of State for Education that for many of the little monsters in her schools there was still – nearly 30 years after the war – precious little in the family cupboard.

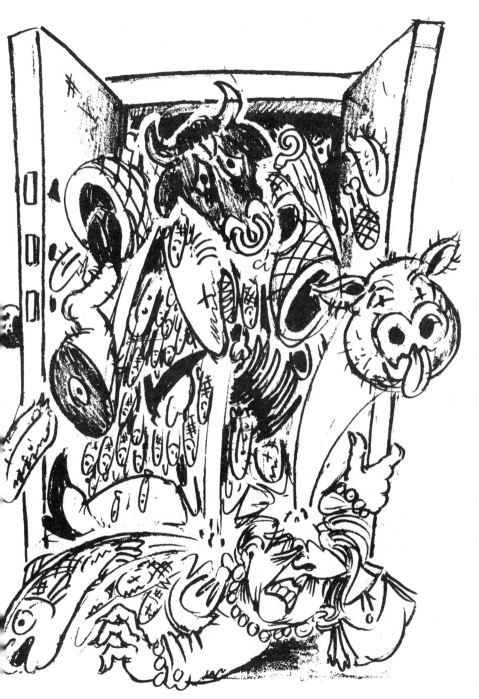

She regretted her gaffe over milk.

'From free school milk to no milk was a big jump – too big a jump. I think we might have put it on sale.'

Even so, Margaret Thatcher had been doing something important. She had been attracting others within the Tory party who, like herself, felt out of touch with the times, whose views seemed old-fashioned, not to say ugly. The sixties was an age of major liberal reforms in Britain, accompanied by commercially successful 'trend setting' permissiveness – mini skirts, pop music, and open sexuality.

Margaret Thatcher stood apart from the majority on virtually every social issue. **'I think the cane has a place in the training of children.'** And she wanted the ROPE. In 1964, 1966 and 1969, she voted for CAPITAL PUNISHMENT.

She also found a man she could trust and admire, someone who would become her political mentor...

ENOCH POWELL

He offered a broad, if stiff shoulder to cry on, and a cup of tea and a chat, when Tory wives ignored her, or when she was rebuffed in Whitehall and Parliament.

Enoch was a forceful personality, a man from the Old School, a man like her father. And more.

Remember Margaret Thatcher's speech in Blackpool in 1968? The boring one?

To Enoch Powell it sounded familiar. He had written much the same some eight years earlier.

Enoch wasn't just an inspiration for a muddled colleague. He had a score to settle. He felt that he was the rightful leader, if not of the Conservative Party, then of its constituency.

Edward Heath was his implacable enemy.

In 1968 Powell had delivered a carefully phrased, and to many a racist, speech to Birmingham businessmen. It was pure classical allegory, heavy in allusions to barbarian invasion, rivers of blood and the Decline and Fall of Empire. The media gave him spectacular coverage.

Heath immediately sacked him from the shadow cabinet.

Six years later, during the 1974 election campaign, Enoch Powell took his revenge. He encouraged people to vote Labour. Enoch seemed to sense there were hundreds of thousands of voters out there who would rally to the call to stamp out 'permissiveness', who would vote Conservative given the 'right' leader.

Despite the Race Relations Act bigotry was still a potent vote catcher.

In 1978, when she was shadow Prime Minister, Margaret Thatcher displayed the qualities for which Powell admired her. Labour government was ahead in the opinion polls. The National Front — Britain's racist bovver-boys — was showing well in the polls too, sapping potential Tory votes.

Margaret Thatcher soon stopped that. Having carefully consulted with her advisors, she appeared on television:

'I think people are really rather afraid that this country might be rather swamped by people with a different culture and, you know, the British character has done so much for democracy and the law, and done so much throughout the world, that if there is any fear that it might be swamped, people are going to be really rather hostile to those coming in.'

It was 'really rather' tasteless. But 'people' took the hint. Her ratings rose dramatically.

National Front members joined the Conservative Party. One became a constituency candidate, apparently with the approval of Conservative Central Office.

Since then Margaret has said very little about race. She simply extols the virtues and values of a bygone imperial Victorian Britain. Party workers do the dirty work, listening with approving nods at doorsteps while voters spit on their neighbours.

Did Margaret Thatcher regret her 'Britain will be swamped' TV statement? Not a bit. Shortly before polling day in 1979, she told a reporter:

'I stand by it 100 per cent. Some people have felt swamped by immigrants. They've seen the whole character of their neighbourhood change — of course people can feel they've been swamped.'

That's Enoch Powell's kind of leader.

MARGARET THATCHER had another teacher. Sir Keith Joseph. His family owned Bovis, the construction group.

He'd had a troubled personal life. And some of his senior colleagues felt that he was obsessive. Nonetheless, Sir Keith has always thought of himself as a passionate moral philosopher.

65

So when he announced in 1974 that the poorest women in Britain threatened the nation because they were breeding too prolifically, he meant it – sincerely.

'The balance of our population, our human stock is threatened,' he said. 'They are producing problem children, the future unmarried mothers, delinquents, denizens of our borstals, sub-normal educational establishments, prisons, hostels for drifters . . . If we do nothing, the nation moves towards degeneration.'

It was a conclusion, he felt, to which anyone with intellectual courage would be drawn. It was the language of Social Darwinists, Malthusians, Eugenicists and disciplinarians of the Victorian era.

'What I most admire about Keith is his first class mind', said Margaret.

Sir Keith had also been thinking about the economy, and the country's leaders.

'The country has been suffering from a running vendetta conducted by the socialists against our free enterprise system and those who manage it. Free enterprise has not failed. We politicians have failed to use it in the framework in which it could have made us prosperous.'

This was balm to Margaret Thatcher, still licking her 'Milk Snatcher' sores. She'd always been distrustful of intellectuals. Yet Sir Keith seemed such a rigorous thinker.

His diagnosis was simple:

'This country – with its inflation, its debts, and its dependence upon foreign credit – no longer has the option of spending its way out of unemployment.'

Incomes policy was not the cure. 'As a way to abate inflation... it is like trying to stop water coming out of a leaky hose without turning off the tap: if you stop the hole it will find two others.'

New medicine was required: a purge on government spending.

'The first period of self-restraint by the Chancellor will be the worst, but it will be the beginning of the cure.'

The treatment lacked but one thing to succeed: getting the doctors into power.

Which meant winning a general election.

Which meant capturing the party leadership.

Which meant dumping Ted Heath.

THE PLOT THICKENS

In 1973 Ted Heath was still Prime Minister. He introduced a series of budgets to expand the economy. But the price of oil suddenly quadrupled after the Arab-Israeli war. And the miners went on strike, closing down power stations.

Prices rocketed. Energy was rationed. Industry closed down to a three day week. It was bloody cold.

Ted Heath called an election in early 1974. But the public didn't like living without lights and heating during the winter. Some listened to Enoch Powell. Heath packed his bags and Harold Wilson returned to Downing Street.

But Heath was still leader of the Tory Party. And Conservative Central Office was still packed with his loyal supporters.

Sir Keith planned a coup.

First, he got together a gaggle of right wing fellow travellers – mostly economists and journalists. Then he coolly suggested to Heath that he set up a little study group with party funds just around the corner. Nothing fancy; just an office where a few friends could discuss 'long range policy'. Heath – a decent chap – agreed. Sir Keith got a brass nameplate and door knocker – and called it the Centre for Policy Studies.

Margaret Thatcher was his vice-chairperson.

It proved even better than a ministry.

Other Tory MPs too, were dissatisfied with their leader. Through their caucus, the 1922 Committee, they asked Heath to stand for RESELECTION.

'Wait a minute. Isn't that what Labour MPs have to do with their constituency parties?'

Yes.

'And isn't that a bit militant?'

Indeed.

The question was who would run against him. Sir Keith had the only organised opposition to the party. But he wasn't a suitable candidate to be British Prime Minister.

Margaret Thatcher, on the other hand, was still relatively unknown. She'd be a possible 'compromise' candidate who might let the party's barons push her around. So she walked into Heath's office and announced her candidature.

He was annoyed but not impressed.

Nevertheless Margaret found eager supporters.

Airey Neave was one. He'd been one of her few friends when they were in law chambers together.

During the war he'd escaped from Colditz, the Nazi prison camp, and then organized escape routes across occupied Europe for British saboteurs. He easily became a Tory MP. Civilian life didn't really suit him. But he was game for intrigue.

Airey Neave became one of Margaret Thatcher's campaign managers, dragging weak-kneed Tories into corners of Parliament and stiffening their backbones in the Members' Bar.

Then, the night before the crucial ballot, Independent TV gave Margaret Thatcher a half hour of prime viewing time to explain 'Why I want to be Leader'

'That was nice of them.'

She won. It was 11 February 1975.

ET TU, MAGGIE?

Margaret Thatcher soon acquired a taste for power. She liked it. And wanted more.

Tory bigwigs who thought she would defer to them were snubbed. A curious new crowd took over Conservative Central Offices. Fringe figures crept from the woodwork of the political right and came out for the first time into the limelight. They were grateful to be given a hearing. And flattered in return. They too were peddling that ostensibly new brand of political soap – Monetarism.

Milton Friedman and his wife Rose were popular in the US press and on TV chat shows for arguing the virtues of Free Enterprise. They were soon to publish their collected thoughts in the best-selling *Free to Choose*.

'Better government is less government.'

'Governments don't help the poor', they said.

It was as American as apple pie, the sort of cracker barrel economics that appealed to Margaret Thatcher. And Milt, after all, had been a professor at the University of Chicago, and a Nobel Prize-winner. He was also a bit of a political advisor.

In 1964 he advised Barry Goldwater during the Presidential Campaign. Goldwater lost.

Friedman was also welcome in Chile after General Pinochet deposed Salvador Allende's elected socialist government. His Chicago students took key posts in the junta's economics' ministries.

It was to be an experiment in Latin American monetarism — strong government hand in hand with free enterprise.

The junta was a disaster for Chile and democracy.

Bodies turned up on rubbish tips, their thumbs tied with wire, shot in the neck, mutilated. Union leaders, priests, Allende's supporters.

And as for Chile's new monetarist policies?

Instead of competitive business booming, the military grabbed what it could.
Generals became monopolists.
Inflation skyrocketed.
Banks went bust.
And unemployment was horrendous.

Friedman said he hated the violence. But he also said:

'Those are old students of mine down there and I'll be goddamned if I'm going to turn my back on them.'

Milton Friedman had a bagful of cures for Britain too.

'Britain has cancer,' he told the *Daily Mail* in 1976. 'The most important thing is to tell the patient, and then to do something drastic. The most drastic thing you can do is to cut every single programme of government spending by 10 per cent, right across the board . . . No promises to do it a year from now . . . Simply announce a straight cut across the board.'

And cut taxes.
Abolish exchange controls.
Sell off nationalized industries, and
make people pay on demand for social services.

What Britain needed was a strong government with guts.

Margaret Thatcher thought he was terrific!

As did Rose, Friedman's wife. 'My husband is against minimum wages. Some people say: 'How terrible! Friedman would like to see teenagers getting only 25 cents an hour.' Well, his argument is: at least this way they can be at work. Now is that heartless? Or reality?'

Friedman also claimed to have discovered the secret of economic policy. He agreed with Sir Keith. Don't bother with incomes policies. Or protracted and complex negotiations. Or planned, coordinated production for national economic priorities.

Chuck them in the bin.

All the government had to do was instruct the Treasury and the Bank of England to squeeze the amount of money in circulation. And . . .

The portals of Economic Freedom would open up. There would be lower inflation . . . So people would lower their expectations . . . They would become 'more realistic' as to what they needed to earn to be able to buy what they needed to live . . . Wages would decrease . . . And profits would go up, up, up.

It all seemed marvellously simple – too simple by half. But Friedman had packaged it as something intellectually new and brand-named it Monetarism. The pundits of Britain's financial press were agog.

Margaret Thatcher bought it lock, stock and barrel. It was to mean that a shopkeeper's daughter as Prime Minister, with a lawyer and then an ex-journalist as her treasury ministers, could determine Britain's economic policy with little regard to the views of their cabinet colleagues, or to the professional economists and technocrats who play major roles in shaping the policies of Europe, Japan and America.

And what Friedman couldn't deliver, Margaret Thatcher picked up from Friedrich von Hayek, a septuagenarian Austrian anti-communist. He'd won a Nobel Prize too.

Von Hayek's most memorable wheeze has been to blame unemployment entirely on the trade unions.

'The people who prevent the unemployed from getting a job are the employed who will not allow them to work for less than the wages currently determined by the unions.'

Clever, isn't it? If you believe this, you can argue that government policies have no effect on the market for jobs. And even better, that Margaret Thatcher and her deflationary policies cannot be blamed for the growing dole queues.

Such is the wonderful strength of dogma.

From a small office near Parliament – the Institute of Economic Affairs – von Hayek's tracts were pressed into the hands of politicians. The Institute's staff became among her most eager advisors, helping her to memorise their arguments. Once in office she gonged some of them.

But what about the Russians?

'Well, what about them?'

Margaret Thatcher had absolutely no foreign policy experience.

That didn't matter.

Professional Cold Warriors – journalists, 'defence specialists', and a group calling itself the National Association For Freedom – quickly offered their services. They saw KGB spies and dupes everywhere: under the bed, on the bed, between the sheets, everywhere. So in 1976 when she needed to get something on the record about the Russians, she got it.

'The Russians are bent on world domination,' she thundered. 'They put guns before butter, while we put just about everything before guns. If we cannot draw the lesson . . . then we are destined – in their words – to end up on the scrap heap of history.'

The Press took notice. The Russians dubbed her 'The Iron Lady'. Margaret Thatcher was aflutter.

'Ladies and Gentlemen,' she told her Finchley constituency party. **'I stand before you tonight in my red chiffon evening gown, my face softly made up, my hair gently waved. The Iron Lady of the Western World! Me? A Cold Warrior?'**

MAY 1979. Labour Prime Minister James Callaghan called a general election.

The Tory campaign couldn't have been easier. They splashed pictures of dole queues on bill boards across the nation, and wrote under them, 'Labour Isn't Working.' For this the Tories paid good money to Saatchi and Saatchi, the party's advertising agency.

In fact Sunny Jim and his Chancellor Dennis Healey had been wholeheartedly squeezing the economy in line with the International Monetary Fund's conditions for supporting the pound. They had even introduced 'cash limits' on government spending. It was a mild deflation and it seemed to be working.

Inflation was falling. There was some growth. Much of the cost was being borne by workers and their families as services were cut and unemployment rose.

What more could a businessman want?

A lot. Union leaders were too welcome at Downing Street to make employers happy. And even then Sunny Jim demonstrably couldn't control the rank-and-file.

Instead of calling an election in autumn 1978 – which he stood a good chance of winning – he tried to stay in office and hold public sector workers' pay rises to 5 per cent.

That winter they went on strike.

Hospitals turned away patients.
Dustbins remained unemptied.
Refuse clogged the streets.

The press made a meal of it. So did Margaret Thatcher.

Companies also took the hint. Instead of building factories and creating jobs from Grimsby to Port Talbot, they stashed their money away in the banks, which were paying an attractive rate of interest. This further intensified the investment squeeze on Callaghan's graceless government.

The Conservatives romped home. With promises of tax cuts and rates held steady, they won crucial votes among working class families who had recently moved to the suburbs and who needed to keep up payments on the car, the video and the mortgage. Council tenants welcomed the Tory promise to sell them their homes.

'It is important that young couples purchase their own home as early as possible. The chances are that they will never then come to be dependent on the state.'

Thousands of Labour supporters, fed up with their government, simply refused to vote.

IN COMMAND

When she moved into Downing Street, Margaret Thatcher changed the furnishings. Then she abolished exchange controls.

Out went Socialism. In came Free Enterprise.

There was champagne in the board rooms, bouquets and kisses in the City of London.

Margaret Thatcher wasted no time in showing who was in charge. The country was in for lashings of her medicine.

AFTER HOGARTH

BUDGET ONE – JUNE 1979

A shot in the arm for electoral supporters: top-rated income tax down from 83 to 60 per cent, civil servants' salaries up one quarter.

Which meant the rest of the country had to swallow the pill. VAT doubled on everything from light bulbs to soap flakes.

There was also some surgery. Without the benefit of anaesthetics.

£3.5 billion chopped from public spending, with subsidies withdrawn from several nationalized industries.

After-care was simple: fatten up the healthy (as long as they were in the private sector) and starve the 'parasites' (as long as they were publicly owned).

How fared the patient?

'Aaargh!!!'

In less than a year inflation rose to 21.9 per cent, interest rates shot to 17 per cent.

The country's economy was sicker than ever. The doctor's verdict?

'After almost any major operation, you feel worse before you convalesce. But you do not refuse the operation when you know that, without it, you will not survive.'

Part of the problem was the Chancellor – Sir Geoffrey Howe. A decent lawyer and dedicated to his leader, he was strictly an amateur in economics and seemingly hopeless with figures.

'Debating with him is about as exciting as being savaged by a dead sheep,' said Dennis Healey.

'Onward, Geoffrey.'

BUDGET TWO – MARCH 1980.

A large dose of snake oil.

The Treasury had worked out a cure – a Medium Term Financial Strategy. If public expenditure was repeatedly bled over several years, then the economy – what was left of it – would be 'lean and fit' and in the private sector. With the money supply in check and a progressively lower Public Sector Borrowing Requirement, inflation too would be cured.

'Scalpel please, Geoffrey.'

Some £13 billion was to come out of the economy.

And how was the patient?

'Aaargh!!!'

Three months later the high interest rates had attracted so much money to London that the pound rose to $2.40. Speculators made a killing. With the City of London awash with dollars and revenue from North Sea oil, the money supply grew faster in two months than it was supposed to for the whole year.

But the rest of the economy was in a coma.

British business competitiveness overseas was nearly wiped out. Unemployment reached 2 million for the first time since 1935. ICI, Britain's largest corporation, declared its first ever trading loss.

'Surely there was some mistake, doctor?'

Not a bit.

'We have started, we have cut government spending considerably, we are controlling the money supply. The immediate effect of that, I am afraid, is increased interest rates, just as sometimes the immediate effect of an antibiotic can be rather damaging to your digestive system.'

Margaret Thatcher kept insisting that the patient's failure to recover was due to its having caught the cold of 'world recession'. Yet Britain's performance was worse than that of any other Western nation.

'Go get 'em, Geoffrey.' And he did.

MINI-BUDGET — NOVEMBER 1980

The economy was having convulsions. But the doctor too was having problems. He was running short of cash to pay for the surgery.

So Sir Geoffrey GRABBED!

£2 billion more in taxes for the Treasury from the North Sea Oil and National Insurance Surcharges.

And CHOPPED!

Another £1 billion off public expenditure.

'It's like a nurse looking after a sick patient. Which is the better nurse? The one who smothers the patient with sympathy and says, "Never mind dear; there, there, you just lie back and I'll bring you all your meals." Or the nurse who says, "Now come on, shake your self out of it. I know you've had an operation yesterday. It's time you took a few steps. That's right dear, that's right. Now get back and take a few more tomorrow." Which is the one most likely to get the results? The one who says "Come on, you can do it." That's me.'

Then, with both output falling and unemployment rising faster than at any time since the end of the Second World War, Sir Geoffrey introduced...

BUDGET THREE – MARCH 1981.

Amputation!

The Public Sector Borrowing Requirement was to be slashed by £3 billion during the year. The government needed cash transfusions fast. Taxes went up.

By spring 1982, only three years after Margaret Thatcher had been elected, world trade was growing and inflation was finally coming down. But while Britain's imports had risen by two fifths, exports remained stagnant. Manufacturing output had even *fallen* by one fifth (almost three times more than any other industrialized country).

And unemployment?

'We are somewhere near the plateau, near the top,' said Normal Tebbit, Employment Secretary.

But 'we' weren't. Unemployment rose by more than 100,000 a month, to over 3 million by March 1983. It had risen by more than 2 million since Margaret Thatcher came to power, but she remained undaunted.

'If ever a Conservative government starts to do what it knows to be wrong because it is afraid to do what it is sure is right, then that's the time for Tories to cry stop. You'll never need to do that while I'm Prime Minister.'

Yet there was a bit of a problem. Monetarism, after all, was supposed to create *growth*. To all appearances it hadn't. Even Milton Friedman was unhappy. He felt the government's passion for reducing the Public Sector Borrowing Requirement was out of all proportion to other needed measures. So much so that *she* was giving *his* monetarism a bad name.

'Oh, it's more important than that,' his wife Rose pitched in. 'It's lead to the idea that monetarism has failed.'

Indeed it had.

'Margaret Thatcher is doing for monetarism what the Boston Strangler did for door-to-door salesmen,' said Dennis Healey.

The Bank of England had some experts take a cool look at Friedman's figures. Particularly for ALIKAZAMM!, the fundamental monetarist proposition that the growth of inflation parallels the growth of the money supply. Friedman claimed the relationship held for both Britain and the United States for most of this century.

In October 1983, the Bank's experts published their results. Friedman's claims were bunkum.

'The failure to present test evidence pertinent to their main assertions leaves these devoid of credibility.'

'Almost every assertion in the book is false,' added one of the report's authors.

The monetarist game was up.

The experience could have embarrassed a lesser man or woman. But not Margaret Thatcher. Her cure had been deeply faulted, both in theory and practice. But never mind.

She just changed the doctor.

Out went shuffling Sir Geoffrey. And in came his number two at the Treasury, ex-journalist Nigel Lawson, who pushed on with more of the same medicine.

Nigel, an ambitious man, needed no prodding.

'There is no doubt that Britain is on the road to recovery,' he wrote with touching optimism in the *News of the World* soon after becoming Chancellor.

Yet to the growing dismay of much of the country, sensible people, and even his colleagues, it wasn't.

HOW DOES SHE GET AWAY WITH IT?

● Simple. Sack the critics!

'As Prime Minister I couldn't waste time having any internal arguments.'

Norman St. John-Stevas. He gets on well with the Queen Mother and was Minister for the Arts. A man of high Tory compassion. And also a bit of a wit. He called Margaret Thatcher 'The Immaculate Misconception.'

5 January 1981. Sack him!

Sir Ian Gilmour: Lord Privy Seal and Deputy Foreign Secretary. An intellectual. And 'wet'. So 'wet you could shoot snipe off him,' said a friend.

'There has been a temptation in some quarters to go back to the 19th century in search of allegedly eternal truths,' he protested, 'instead of dealing with present day realities.'

14 September 1981. Sack him!

Said Gilmour, 'It does no harm to throw the occasional man overboard, but it does not do much good if you are steering full speed ahead for the rocks.'

Then came **Gordon Richardson**. He was Governor of the Bank of England, and had the temerity to talk back to Margaret Thatcher. More than that, he kept wanting to bring down interest rates. And seems not to have stopped the clearing banks from quietly lending money to several of Britain's major companies which were heading for disaster.

Horrors!

Well, it was to Margaret Thatcher. It appeared that the Bank of England was not following her instructions to squeeze the money supply. So when Richardson's term of office expired, in July 1983, he was promptly shown the door. His place was taken by one of her least reticent City admirers.

The faint-hearted fell like nine pins. Carlisle, Pym, Prior... Since 1981 Margaret Thatcher has surrounded herself within the cabinet almost entirely with 'yes-men' and cronies.

● And she was especially lucky. She had been blessed with a self-cannibalising opposition – a Labour Party which busily ripped itself apart, leaving her a near free hand to do much as she pleased with the country.

First Denis Healey and Tony Benn slugged it out for the party's deputy leadership. Then a group of Labour MPs who'd never got on well with the unions and felt uncomfortable with nuclear disarmament, walked out and set up the Social Democratic Party. This left the Labour Party largely to union bosses brawling with local constituency groups keen to introduce a bit of comradely democracy.

But Margaret Thatcher still needed something more than a fractured and impotent parliamentary opposition to secure a second term. By early 1982 the public couldn't see her promised **'light at the end of the tunnel'**.

● The Falklands war soon changed that. Margaret and Victory became synonymous.

'In a way the Falklands became my life, it became my bloodstream.'

In fact, she had herself inadvertently precipitated it. In early 1982 the *HMS Endurance*, the ship which patrolled the Falkland Islands, was to be recalled from the South Atlantic – yet another victim of spending cuts. British intelligence, even Jim Callaghan, cautioned against it. But Sunny Jim was an old navy man, and Margaret was keen to keep the Argentine junta happy – the trade in Argentine corned beef and British armaments was just too lucrative.

In mid-March she gave a Queen's Award for Export Achievement to British Manufacture and Research Corporation, Grantham's munitions firm, for selling anti-aircraft weaponry to Argentina. These were to work with devastating effect against Colonel H's paratroopers at Goose Green.

What more could Argentina's generals and admirals have wanted?

On Wednesday, March 31, Margaret Thatcher knew that invasion was imminent. But she waited until Friday April 2, after the British garrison on the Falklands had surrendered, before telling the House of Commons. The next day Michael Foot surrendered as well. He offered his unqualified support to Margaret Thatcher. From then on it was political plain sailing.

'Do you remember what Queen Victoria said? Failure? The possibility does not exist.'

A public opinion poll in February 1982 gave her 30 per cent of the vote. A poll shortly after the war gave her 45%.

'Rejoice! Rejoice!'

'I'm not going to dwell on the Falklands factor,' she said.

Oh?

Conservative Rally, Cheltenham. July 1982.

'Why does it need a war to bring out our qualities and reassert our pride?'

Conservative Party Conference, Brighton. October 1982.

'This is not going to be a speech about the Falklands Campaign although I would be proud to make one.'

The *Daily Mail*. August 1982.

'At times the woman they call the Iron Lady shed tears for the young men who were dying. "You can't help it. They just come. But you pull yourself together very quickly, you have to." '

The Archbishop of Canterbury was similarly moved. At the Memorial Service in St Paul's Cathedral he prayed for the war dead — all the dead, Argentinians included. Sitting in the congregation, Margaret Thatcher was livid.

The Archbishop should have known that God wears a Union Jack.

In the election the next year, Michael Foot was Labour's candidate for Prime Minister. Though a noted rhetorician, as a leader he proved hopelessly weak and ineffectual. He was also lumbered with a 10,000 word manifesto — a jumbo bag of political all-sorts, promising everything to everyone depending on race, sex or creed.

'The longest suicide note in history,' quipped Denis Healey.

The Conservatives won easily. Once again many Labour supporters simply didn't bother to vote, and the new Social Democratic-Liberal Alliance attracted millions of middle-of-the-roaders. But they didn't count as British elections are run on the principle of first past the post.

With fewer than one in three of the electorate voting Conservative, she won a majority of 144 seats in the House of Commons. It was the largest majority – and on one of the smallest shares of the vote – since the war.

Which was just as well, from Margaret Thatcher's point of view, because by then she was in hot water.

The cost of keeping the unemployed and pensioners in ciggies and chips, and their kids from rioting too often, was costing more in 'benefits' than was 'saved' from cuts in public expenditure. She had already trimmed pensions, raised prescription charges and cut (and then *taxed*) unemployment benefit.

'I believe it was right to cut the increase in unemployment benefits because it is right to have a large difference between those in work and those out of work.'

Yet the Treasury was still strapped for cash.

North Sea oil revenue helped. Instead of investing in new industry, Margaret Thatcher simply used it to top up the government's current account to pay for day to day spending. She was widely criticised for not putting to better purpose one of the nation's most welcome (and short-lived) assets, but she was unbowed.

'We reject the socialist view that oil revenues should be retained by the Government and used to increase state power by state intervention in industry. Instead we believe that this provides us with a means of reducing still further the necessary evil of personal taxation, so that once again it pays to work to acquire skill and to take a risk.'

Yet even the North Sea bonanza wasn't enough to cover the massively increased social expenditure created by her deflationary policies. So Margaret seized on an obvious, if to many a characteristically extreme solution. She too stripped the shop.

She sold off nationalised industries to raise more cash for the Treasury's kitty, then plundered the social services by selling off what could be turned to a profit while running down the rest.

'We must never allow state monopoly to replace competition, or collectivism to strangle individual endeavour. Let this be an era of enterprise.'

From another perspective she was ordering the largest redistribution of wealth within Britain since Henry VIII dissolved the monasteries. But with a difference: while Henry confiscated the church's property on behalf of his state, Margaret Thatcher sold off the public domain held in trust by her government. And at cut-rate prices.

Nigel Lawson, as First Secretary to the Treasury and then as Chancellor, dumped public property and business into private hands as fast as he could.

The scale of the transfer has been truly prodigious. Some £10 billion of national capital assets alone floated on the stock market.

Among the first to go was Amersham International, the government's manufacturer of radio-active isotopes.

Then Cable and Wireless, Associated British Ports and British Aerospace.

And the British Sugar Corporation, the National Freight Company and Britoil.

David Owen, the SDP leader, had privately mooted the possibility of *giving* the shares to the public, who after all owned the nationalized industries in the first place. But Margaret Thatcher would have none of it.

In 1984 the first sale of British Telecom shares netted the government £1.5 billion.

'It was the largest share issue ever to be brought to the market on either side of the Atlantic, some 2 million people bought shares. This is what capitalism is – a system which brings wealth to many and not just a few.'

It is also a system which has brought tens of millions of pounds to brokers in agents' fees, and windfall profits to small investors when the shares they had just bought at knockdown prices were immediately gobbled up by the big financial institutions.

'We need to create a mood where it is everywhere morally right for as many people as possible to acquire capital.'

She did that all right. Counting up their quick profits made on British Telecom shares, small investors bayed for the government to float more on the market at similarly low prices.

It's an expensive way to buy votes, especially as Britain's little capitalists have been holding out for more government give-aways instead of investing in other – cash-starved – British industries.

People who can't afford shares have been encouraged to buy their council homes. And millions have, enabling Nigel Lawson to write off some £1.5 billion a year from the government's housing ledger. The costs are now borne by the new owners as private mortgages. Which, of course, is long term personal debt – on which compound interest in payable. The banks and building societies couldn't be happier. They know that mortgaged homes are the tied cottages of the 1980s.

So does Margaret Thatcher.

That's why she wants a nation of home owners, snug and comfy, able to shed an occasional glycerine tear for the unemployed neighbour. And as for council tenants, turned owners, who become unemployed and can no longer afford the payments?

That's their problem, isn't it.

Margaret Thatcher had made a promise to fill people's pockets by cutting their taxes, and she was going to stick to it. But the government still needed that income. So instead of taking money from people's pay packets, Nigel Lawson loaded taxes on to things they bought. This gives the illusion of greater disposable incomes, before the Treasury carves off its slice.

Since 1979, taxes on gas, on electricity, on water, on postage, on telephone calls, have gone up, and up, and up.

Then by squeezing central funding to local authorities for maintaining roads, parks, schools and other basic amenities and services, the tax burden has been shifted on to local rates. By 1985 British tax payers were paying *more* in taxes under the Tories than they had in 1979, under the Labour government.

So much for her promised tax cuts, and the unleashing of 'individual endeavour'.

As for dismantling the 'growing "state monopolies" smothering competition'... there have been problems too. Many of these state institutions have been difficult to privatize, largely because they're not very profitable — schools, hospitals, community services, parks and municipal maintenance. And many of these are not products of so-called post-war 'Socialism'. They are the inheritance left by farsighted planners of the Victorian era.

Nonetheless, Margaret and her ministers didn't flinch. They know that while such amenities can't be sold in their entirety, there are plenty of tasty morsels within them just waiting to be prised out. So Margaret Thatcher has simply squeezed her own government, while giving entrepreneurs a leg up.

While state schools have been short of chalk and books, grants and tax credits have been pumped into private education. Although hospitals have been closed, private insurance schemes have provided the wherewithal for private clinics. As the most heavily travelled bus routes have been opened to private firms, many of those to remote villages have been withdrawn, along with post offices, telephone boxes, and road repairs. Hospital laundry, school meals and garbage collection have gone out to private tender.

And the result?

For those who can afford them, private schools, private clinics and comfortable pensions.

And for the rest?

QUEUES

Queues such as haven't been seen in Britain since war-time rationing. They're not like the ones in Eastern Europe, though. In Britain there are no queues for meat or jeans or cars. Anyone can buy them, at any time. If you've got the money, of course.

In Britain there are queues –

At the Post Office, when you're collecting dole money or your pension.

And in the doctor's waiting room, the hospital out-patients clinic, and for an operation.

At social security offices.

And when you hear of a job.

Does it hurt?

You bet.

Doctors, nurses, teachers and other public servants don't like hearing their training, dedication and years of hard work dismissed – with the sweep of a phrase – as mere 'inefficiency' and 'restrictive practice'. Or of jobs lost and not replaced, as 'shake out', as if workers are so much dirt; or 'natural wastage', as if they're something even filthier.

It also hurts families to see kidney patients die for want of surgery or access to a machine, children's wards closed, school kids in overcrowded classrooms who can't read, and pensioners skimping on heating to buy a few strips of bacon.

Critics say that in the society Margaret Thatcher is making, those who cannot afford to pay will be ignored. But she says that's unfair.

They've forgotten charity.

As she explained, looking back longingly to the Victorian era:

'As people prospered themselves, so they gave voluntarily things to the state. So many of the schools we replace were voluntary schools, so many of the hospitals we replace were given by this great benefaction feeling we have in Britain, even some of the prisons, some of the town halls.'

Have you felt the 'benefaction feeling' of providing prisons?

It doesn't matter. Margaret Thatcher's simply marched the country backwards, restructuring the entire nation around her father's grocery-counter values. And just as in his day, she's surrounded by a massive pool of unskilled and under-employed on the look out for work even at lower wages, prepared to do half jobs, bits of jobs, anything for a few bob to keep body and soul together. If you're black, young or a woman, you're probably worse off than others.

Her problem is that they're not all forelock tuggers.

In the absence of full time jobs paying decent wages, the more resourceful have turned to odd jobs and moon-lighting. And quick money – un-taxed – is to be had in street crime; nowhere faster than in burglary and the drugs traffic.

The police have been beefed up to keep a lid on the inner cities. And when inevitably the kids boil over, Margaret Thatcher throws some money into the ghettoes – while simply blaming 'criminals' for the damage.

It's hardly surprising that Britain now produces the most exceptional football hooligans and riots in Europe.

There are, of course, smatterings of clever young men and women working with computers. But most school leavers simply don't have the skills and techniques needed to work in modern industry. Alongside their Japanese, German and Italian counterparts, Britain's kids are technological illiterates.

It takes a certain type of person to advocate Thatcherism. What other Prime Minister would have had as Secretary of State for Education a man who actually believes that his greatest responsibility, at a time when children desperately need new skills and teachers are miserable, is to fight a war against the so-called 'bully boys of the left' in the universities. A man who, frankly, seems a bit of an hysteric.

'Are we to be destroyed from the inside, too, a country which successfully repelled and destroyed Philip of Spain, Napoleon, the Kaiser, Hitler?'

And her Employment Secretary, now party chairman, Norman Tebbit.

'On the whole, youngsters are pretty resilient. Those going into sixth forms at the moment, some of them my son's contemporaries, are very much looking towards the market for their skills.'

Try saying that in Brixton, Toxteth, Newcastle or Tower Hamlets.

And Nigel Lawson, her belt-tightening Chancellor:

'I cut things out altogether. My holidays are now very much less lavish. I have almost cut out eating in restaurants – I used to enjoy that a great deal but I think it's an absurd extravagance – and I can't bear to eat in an inferior restaurant.'

These are the stalwarts.

There are also the embarrassments. Her nearest and dearest who seem to think they need not be judged as she and they would judge others.

Mark Thatcher, for instance.

A problem child. No genius. But his mother loves him.

He had a string of lousy jobs, until she became Prime Minister. Then he too moved into Downing Street and set up business. He took a job with his mother's tycoon friend, Lord Victor Matthews, who owned the *Daily Express* and much else besides. Mark quietly hustled contracts for Matthews's overseas building company, Cementation International.

So when Margaret Thatcher was in Oman on an official visit in 1981, trying to sell a British-built university to the sultan... Mark was there too. Matthews's firm got the contract – which never went out to tender – worth some £300 million. And Mark got a commission, part of which went into the bank account he shared with his father.

Three years later, when the *Observer* newspaper found out, his mother retreated into stony silence. As she told the House of Commons:

'I hope we have not reached a stage where parents and sons have to report everything to the authorities. If it comes to that, 1984 will be here.'

So much for the claims of public office.

Then there was Cecil Parkinson, Margaret's favourite cabinet minister, who couldn't keep his hands off his secretary, Sara Keays. When she became pregnant with his child, she insisted on having it.

'Bravo!'

Think again. Sara had been led to believe that Cecil would divorce his wife and marry her, but he had chickened out. Margaret Thatcher advised him to keep it quiet; he stayed in the government.

'How could I possibly have not stood by him, and not allowed him the possibility of continuing his career.'

The *Times* said Cecil had 'made a sad and silly blunder', which seemed to refer to Sara's child. The *Daily Telegraph* asked whether 'a quiet abortion' might not have been preferable.

'I am not aware that political expediency was sufficient grounds for an abortion under the 1967 Act,' retorted Sara.

She also said Cecil had asked her to marry him a second time, then backed off yet again after a holiday with his family. Now Cecil had gone too far. The British don't mind a politician who sleeps with his secretary, or even a cad, but it won't do to have a cabinet minister who's so colossally muddle-headed.

For her own part, Margaret Thatcher's never made any pretence of believing in anything other than the good old double standard. In her natural order of things, some people deserve special treatment.

'**What is opportunity if your only opportunity is to be equal?**... **I do not believe it is in the character of the British people to begrudge the lion's share to those who have genuinely played the lion's part.**'

'**As for being out of touch with ordinary people, that's just nonsense,**' she told a newspaper shortly before she became Prime Minister. '**People know I have a sizeable house in the country, and they confuse size with wealth. I don't mind telling you that the house I wanted was several thousand pounds more than the one we got.**'

So in August 1985, without batting an eyelid, she announced a 48 per cent pay rise for admirals, generals, high court judges and senior civil servants. The House of Lords, fastidious in its privileges, finally threw it out, not wishing to be tarred with so crude a brush on so desolate a social canvas.

Is it surprising that Margaret Thatcher's always been in need of some deft repackaging? Let's not beat around the bush. She's required the biggest political remodelling job in Western Europe.

When she became Tory party leader in 1975 she was awkward, frumpish, and uncomfortably aggressive. So Gordon Reece, a record company executive whose firm was used to transforming tuneless youths into top of the pop stars, sat down with her every morning and taught her how to shine in front of the media. But that was only for starters. The collected genius of modern public relations and advertising was summoned to her.

Their verdict? Whole-body cosmetic surgery was called for.

Teeth — *terrible.*

Cap them.

Hair — *going grey.*

Tint it blond. See the hairdresser at least twice a week.

'Keep the hair simple, higher, more off the face.'

Clothing — *appalling.*

Chuck out the tired Tory blues. Make them more feminine. Cut down on jewellery.

Accent — *the worst.*

The impossible Grantham girl aping the upper orders, her haughty oyster in the nose tone. Voice lessons, humming exercises from the National Theatre's trainer.

'Bring down the pitch. Stand closer to microphones... Seem more intimate... Relax, relax, Margaret. You're still too shrill.'

Image — *too cold, austere.*

Photo calls washing up, walkabouts in supermarkets, talks about fashion: 'womanly things.'

Then there are her mannerisms – the clutch in the throat, the eyelid flutter of sincerity, the mock coyness.

With practised disingenuousness, they're delivered with brittle certainty. Speeches go through scores of drafts, written like corporate projects. Even answers to Parliamentary Questions are rehearsed beforehand. In fact the Public Relations entourage has been lucky. The *Sun*, *Daily Mail*, *Daily Express*, *Daily Telegraph*, *News of the World*, have fawned over her. Editors have collected knighthoods. For lowly journalists it has been reward enough to be blessed with an 'exclusive' audience. The humble hacks, in turn, tend to agree with her; they seldom interrupt, contradict, or ask embarrassing questions.

In the trade it's called the 'Prayer Mat Interview'.

And it creates the desired effect: A leader beyond the reach of doubt, except those so carefully chosen she can raise and resolve them without a moment's anxiety in her audience. And beyond question, except those she chooses to ask (and answer) for herself.

Thanks to the press the British public has not only to live with Margaret Thatcher's economic policies, but within her moral universe.

'Economics are the method; the object is to change the heart and soul'

It's not so easy though to 'change the heart and soul' of foreigners. They have an unnerving habit of seeing the world from their own perspectives, not the one from Downing Street's press office.

In foreign affairs, Margaret Thatcher's definitely small beer. She's survived on a string of moral imperatives packaged for home consumption and newspaper headlines. In the field she's put in a less than convincing performance, encompassing costly compromises, a few lies and some out and out failures.

No more than one expects from any politician?

Decide for yourself.

The Russians are an easy target for the occasional tongue lashing. Her more pressing concern, though, has been to keep Britain marching in step behind American priorities, at an escalating cost to tax payers' pockets, sensibilities and even sovereignty.

Margaret Thatcher is nothing if not a generous ally.

She offered to buy American nuclear reactors and Trident submarines – shots in the arm to America's power and defence industries.
Purged the unions from GCHQ, the Cheltenham eavesdropping electronic spy centre.
Welcomed cruise missiles before anyone else in Europe.
Signed over large tracts of countryside to US military jurisdiction.
And enthused about Star Wars.

And what does Britain get in return?

A few minor defence contracts and warm thanks from the president.

'We are very fortunate to have someone else's weapons stationed on our soil to fight those targeted against us... We are the true peace movement.'

Defenders of the Free World can't be faint-hearted. So Michael Heseltine, her Minister of Defence, valiantly rubbished the anti-nuclear movement, the Campaign for Nuclear Disarmament. He dutifully insinuated that CND has been packed with defeatists, dupes and spies, without producing any evidence. He even smiled for the cameras as hapless British squaddies strung barbed wire to keep their fellow citizens out of America's nuclear bases.

There are, it seems, people who like a minister to show a bit of muscle.

Yet Tarzan – as even his friends call him – had trouble with women.

With Sarah Tisdall, a young civil servant who leaked his plans to mislead Parliament about cruise missiles. That cost her six months in jail.

And the women of Greenham Common who repeatedly offered to debate with him.

But he could never make it.

Then there's Ulster. Margaret Thatcher had good reason to feel she was on to a sure winner – 'standing firm' against 'Catholic Irish terrorists'. That, after all, is a longstanding British tradition. And it's a subject on which she is not without passion.

During the 1979 election campaign the Irish National Liberation Army voted just once – with a car bomb, killing Airey Neave.

'Some devil has got him' Margaret Thatcher said. **'They must never, never, never be allowed to triumph. They must never prevail.'**

So she refused to budge when Provisional IRA prisoners went on hunger strike in Long Kesh for political status. And 10 died. The Provos, though, can bear a grudge. In 1984 they tried to bomb her during the Conservative Party Conference, destroying much of the Grand Hotel in Brighton and killing five people. Margaret Thatcher emerged unscathed.

Yet her policy of 'standing firm' has hardly been an unqualified triumph. More than any other British Prime Minister, and probably beyond the IRA's wildest dreams she has succeeded in convincing the Ulster Catholic community that they have no future under British rule. For the first time in Ulster's history, Sinn Fein candidates have won handsomely both local elections and seats in Parliament. A security pact with the Irish Republic, signed late in 1985, was seen as the only way to salvage the situation.

Her greatest strength is that many people in Britain don't give a toss about Ulster. The province is always expected to be a dead end for politicians, a dirty war for soldiers.

And Margaret Thatcher's policies towards the rest of the world?

Among Western European leaders she stands four square behind South Africa's apartheid government, refusing to back sanctions that would bite.

As for the rest of Africa, her government's given less in food aid as a proportion of its resources than any other in Western Europe. Starving Africans would do well to take note of the way in which she reconciles Christianity with the cash till.

'No one would remember the Good Samaritan if he had only had good intentions. He had money as well.'

So while in the long run the meek may inherit the Earth and the righteous may triumph, we are told that for the time being the United States is just this side of paradise.

'She is the last safe haven, everyone's safe haven for their money. She is a very strong enterprising economy. She is never going to have a socialist government. She is the land of freedom, she is the country of last resort and of safe haven for money.'

It's a pity we can't all be bankers.

Only once has Margaret Thatcher come close to becoming seriously unstuck on foreign matters. Over the Falklands, her greatest moment. The question which persists is whether she took decisions which made sure it would happen.

ON 2ND MAY, 1982, at 8pm London time, the nuclear submarine HMS Conqueror torpedoed and sank the vintage Argentine cruiser *General Belgrano*.

GOTCHA!

War hadn't been declared. 368 Argentine sailors died. Whatever chances existed of a peace plan were scuppered and war became inevitable.

Why was the *Belgrano* sunk?

Margaret Thatcher and her ministers have since had trouble finding the answer. First they said that the Belgrano 'posed a very obvious threat – a serious threat' to British forces.

Then they admitted it didn't.

Then they said it 'was close to the total exclusion zone and closing on elements of the task force.'

Then they admitted that it was sailing away from the British fleet back towards Argentina.

Then they said 'the actual decision to launch a torpedo was clearly one taken by the submarine commander.'

Then they admitted that the 'actual' decision to sink the ship was taken by Margaret Thatcher and her war cabinet in London.

And then only after they had changed the rules of engagement to sink any Argentine ship more than 12 miles from Argentina. Without telling the Argentine government.

Perhaps it was inevitable that one of Michael Heseltine's civil servants, a man who wrote ministerial replies for the House of Commons, would feel it was not in his job description to draft lies as well. In any case Clive Ponting, probably one of the few Buddhists in the Ministry of Defence, posted much of the true story to a pestering Labour MP, Tam Dalyell.

Ponting was soon tried for breaking his vows – the Official Secrets Act. The government insisted that this wasn't political, but the jury threw the case out.

'Scandalous,' cried the press and opposition.

It was. But Margaret Thatcher stood her ground. Within a few months the country was well into the swing of the miners' strike. And that one she also won hands down. She'd planned it well: giving in to the miners' pay demands in the first years of office, while manoeuvring a tough Scottish-American executive, Ian MacGregor, into the chair of the National Coal Board.

MacGregor had a reputation for tough management and union bashing in the American metals industry, a reputation which he enhanced at British Leyland and British Steel. Finally, in March 1984 it was leaked that Cortonwood colliery in Yorkshire was to close, the first of many 'uneconomic' pits to be shut by Ian MacGregor. Thousands were to be thrown on the dole. What was and wasn't 'economic' was later shown to be deeply suspect by the same accountants originally called in to do the sums.

But that didn't matter. MacGregor's strength lay in insisting that he saw no need to consult with the National Union of Mineworkers before the pits were shut. Arthur Scargill, the union's president, rose to the challenge; he called a strike on principle, and refused to hold a national ballot.

Margaret Thatcher wasn't just happy; she was over the rainbow.

Neither the Labour Party nor many trade union leaders felt they could join Scargill. The striking miners were left largely on their own; the union was split; their families had to scavenge for food and fuel. Millions of people dug deep into their pockets and sent them groceries and clothing. But after twelve months the miners had to return to the pits, most of them in debt, many of their colleagues sacked, facing fines or in jail.

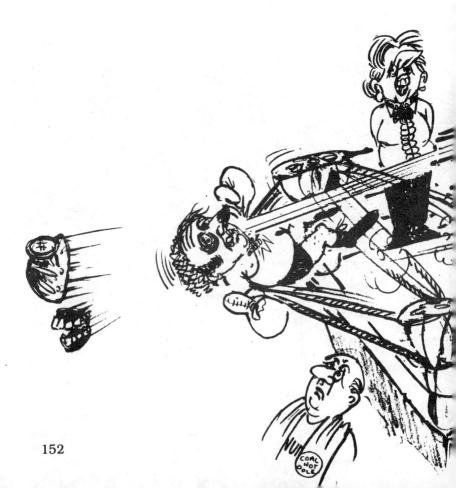

And the bill? That was simply passed to the Exchequer. Some £3.04 million for MacGregor's services rendered. Several million more to bobbies on overtime pushing back pickets. In all, some £2 billion counting lost production and imported coal.

Little was achieved by way of 'improved efficiency', but it certainly bruised and wounded the NUM. And caused plenty of dissension within the Labour Movement. Which can't be bad for starters if you're out to destroy Socialism.

Remember what Margaret Thatcher had said?

'We sacrificed everything in that war [World War Two]. **Then we had Socialism, and it bit very deep into Britain — it bit throughout society.'**

Socialism's teeth had to be pulled; roots, bleeding gums and all. In effect, 'Socialism' had become an all-purpose bogey; a custom-made pretext to scrap or lean on many of Britain's representative and to some extent independent institutions.

Local councils:
Rate capped.
Rate support grants scrapped.

Metropolitan authorities:
Abolished.

Trades unions:
Employment Act 1980
Employment Act 1982
Trade Union Act 1984

The media:
Censor the BBC
Cut its budget.

There was a lot of shouting but little effective resistance.

Oxford University was one of the few institutions which stood up to her. Dons voted overwhelmingly in 1985 not to award her an honorary degree.

In Britain, Margaret Thatcher took this snub in silence. But in the USA she lashed out on TV:

'This is the way socialists work,' she said.

It was asking a lot to be believed, even from Americans. The dons had made it clear that they could not honour an alumnus who had been chopping university teaching and research facilities across the country. Yet Margaret Thatcher has little patience for these finer distinctions. You're either with her, or you're likely to be lumped with Colonel Ghadaffi.

'At one end of the spectrum are the terrorist groups without borders, and the terrorist states who finance and arm them. At the other end are the 'hard left' operating inside our system, conspiring to use union power and the apparatus of local government to break, defy and subvert the laws.'

The truth is that many of Britain's local councillors and local government workers — from Newcastle to deepest Tory Wiltshire — resent being damned by her all-encompassing demonology. From their day to day experience they feel that it is she, and not themselves or even the local unions, who is inflexible, even a bit dictatorial.

And that bothers a lot of other people. According to public opinion polls, by mid-1985 an overwhelming majority of adults in Britain wouldn't vote for Margaret Thatcher were they given the opportunity to do so. Margaret Thatcher had to do something to court popularity. But what?

First she reshuffled the cabinet.

'It's the same old jar of jellybeans,' said David Steel, the Liberal's leader.

So she also announced new policies. To dent the unemployment figures, her minions would create half jobs where there were once full jobs, and then pay the two people working quarter wages.

This is the politics of the vacant lot.

Five years ago there were large, albeit tired, but working industries on those lots. Then they were bulldozed. The men and women who worked them shrank back into the surrounding communities, stayed at home and collected the dole.

Today, pre-fab huts are popping up on those cleared sites. Some are drive-in warehouses full of imported goods. The rest are mostly small businesses run by a manager and a few kids on youth training schemes.

'Look at the good news. Look at the successes.'

And what about the people languishing in the surrounding communities?

'Don't be Moaning Minnies', she told journalists in Newcastle.

Now this is dangerous business. There are millions of voters in those communities.

HORRORS!

Sensible Tories despaired. They know they must win those votes, otherwise they too could be among the ones tending gardens or working as caretakers in City offices after the next election. So Margaret Thatcher told her 'wetter' cabinet ministers to spend some money on social programmes to keep the inner cities quiet. Nigel Lawson would raise it by disposing of the state's remaining assets.

Old Tories, such as Harold Macmillan, described this as nothing less than selling off the family silver.

Yet to Margaret Thatcher's way of thinking, if the government was to be lost to the likes of Neil Kinnock and his 'New Look' Labour Party and/or the Liberal-Social Democratic Alliance, then it was best to make sure that anything of value was in the private sector and leave the dross for government.

In the meantime she would work to improve her image.

'Not again!'

Why not? We live in an age in which public relations calls for heroism. There are knighthoods to be won, gentlemen, not to mention ulcers.

But what more could be done? The hairdo? accent? teeth? dress? Even the pearls had already been restrung.

Ah, yes. But there was still some scope for *gesture*. So Margaret Thatcher quickly:
Hugged a chimp.

Made tea for some girls visiting Downing Street.

And when she visited the Manchester air disaster victims...

'Those who could not speak, I just laid my hand on. I wanted them to know I was there.'

Not bad for starters. But politics has a funny way of catching up with even the most crafty and seasoned of image-makers.

In December 1985, Michael Heseltine had finally had enough. Out of the blue Margaret Thatcher and her Trade minister, Leon Brittan, decided that Britain's only military helicopter firm, Westland, was to be handed over, lock, stock and rotor blade, to the Americans.

This was going too far. Heseltine was Defence secretary, and he wanted a takeover that was more 'European'. But he was ignored. So he stomped out of a cabinet meeting, grabbed the nearest press microphone and announced his resignation. What was left of British sovereignty? he seemed to be asking.

It was then soon discovered that Leon Brittan had leaked a confidential government correspondence to blacken Heseltine's cause; and with the apparent approval of the Prime Minister's office.

Brittan resigned. Margaret Thatcher said she knew nothing of the leak at the time . . . The long shadow of Richard Nixon fell like a pall over her administration.

Since then Margaret Thatcher has again been trying to recast her image. But how many times can she have the operation?

In *The Wizard of Oz*, the Tin Man wept for lack of a heart. Margaret Thatcher's goes back to behind a corner shop counter in Grantham during the Depression when neighbours were sleeping rough in cardboard boxes and her father wouldn't give them anything on tick.

It's a heart weaned on thin, meagre profit margins, and large dollops of righteous indignation.

The Westland affair may have tarnished her image. Nonetheless, Britain is going to be asked to stand up and join Margaret Thatcher to share the spoils of economic victory. Offshore investors will be asked to stump up some cash, to be a little bit patriotic for the Tory party. And voters will be asked to bite their lips, be heroic. She will argue that a vote against her is a return to 'left wing chaos', 'Keynesian cowardice', and savage inflation – in other words, the same old monetarist nightmare.

The trouble is that Britain needs more investment than it has ever had just to keep unemployment from getting even worse, says the Organisation for Economic Cooperation and Development. And oil revenues are falling rapidly.

There is also a whole generation of men and women in their fifties who know that they have been culled: active, capable people who will never work again. And another whole generation – their kids, and their neighbour's kids – who know they have been stunted for life. Money can be kept in a bank collecting interest if it's not put to use. People on the shelf grow poor and angry. They also expect something better.

Margaret Thatcher knows this and that's why she's hedged her bets. She and Denis have already bought their retirement pile. She's also promised the nation that she won't stay as Prime Minister for the full term if re-elected. Yet for many Tory backbenchers that's of little comfort. If she leads her party into the next election they should be in for a trouncing.

Why? Because Margaret Thatcher came to office promising a new 'era of enterprise'. She was given a leg up by businesses, praised by the press, and greeted with widespread popular enthusiasm. But as soon as she was behind the wheel she drove the country smartly into a ditch.

163

Her government has provided the legal basis for major changes in the trades unions. And has sold some council tenants their homes. But what else?

She hasn't 'defeated Socialism'. Instead she's done a lot to damage many people's lives and several of the once-considerable strengths of British capitalism:

Manufacturing industry and the export trade – pillars of Victorian enterprise – all in the doldrums.

Dole queues like nowhere else in Europe and longer than any since the Great Depression.

North Sea oil, the country's one and only windfall bonanza, fast running out, the money spent and with little to show for it.

And finally, the accumulated wealth of Britain's thirty-year post-war economic boom fled overseas with the abolition of exchange controls, for the most part beyond recall.

Her father, Alfred Roberts, was a better shopkeeper.

In 1985 Italy had a higher average standard of living than Britain for the first time in centuries. That's the real achievement of Margaret Thatcher's government.

The British people may be a lot of things, but they're not foolish and they're not blind. Yet because of the electoral system a lot of people are going to have to vote who didn't vote last time. And because the opposition is split between the Labour Party and the Liberal-SDP Alliance a lot of people are going to have to vote intelligently, crossing party lines if need be to get rid of her. (Though the Tories may ditch her first.)

In any case, Britain's next government will have to spend the next years dealing with the damage while Lady Margaret Thatcher holds the House of Lords in thrall and tends to her roses in the suburbs.

GOING FURTHER

Three paperback books:

Margaret Thatcher – Wife, Mother, Politician, by Penny Junor is the best, most readable and intimate biography of Margaret Thatcher available (Sidgwick and Jackson, 1983).

Thatcher's Reign, A Bad Case of the Blues, by Melanie McFadyean and Margaret Renn, is a shrewd and very funny compilation of Margaret Thatcher's idiocies, bloopers and 'wise thoughts' (Chatto and Windus, 1984).

Mrs Thatcher's Economic Experiment, by William Keegan, is a robust and readable analysis of monetarism and Margaret Thatcher's disastrous first term in office wrecking the economy (Penguin Books, 1983).

William Keegan's articles in *The Observer* and Christopher Huhne's in *The Guardian* are highly recommended. They are among Margaret Thatcher's most perceptive critics on economic issues.

There are often detailed reports of the effects of the government's policies in the left press and magazines, including *Marxism Today, New Socialist* and the *New Statesman*, and in City of London business journals and bank reviews.